REPUBLICA SOCIALISTA

ROMÂNIA

D1439341

We had a philosophy class in high school when I was sixteen; that was in 1987. I remember one of the girls asking the teacher what he believed, what church he attended and what denomination he belonged to. He looked very surprised and asked, 'We're all Marxists, aren't we?'

Then some of the girls said that they weren't Marxists, that they were Christians. I was really surprised. They were such nice people that I couldn't understand how they could be Christians. That started arguments and debates in the classroom.

Soon afterwards I heard that the girls had become Christians through attending a Bible study group run by Levente Horvath. I didn't know it then, but Levente would become one of my best friends.

Wrong Type

Very soon after that I started dating one of these girls and her biggest problem was Levente's wife Maria, who told her that she shouldn't go out with a non-Christian. That made me think Christians weren't interested in me because I was the wrong type of person. About then a friend became a Christian through Levente's Bible study group. He and I argued a lot about religion. Eventually my friend arranged for me to visit Levente. I chose to go at night in order that people wouldn't see me.

Maria wasn't at home and Levente was looking after their child. He and I talked for three hours. I was quite impressed, not necessarily with Christianity at that point but with Levente. His basic message was that not all Christians are idiots. My curiosity was raised. He was wise and didn't invite me to join the Bible study group with the other teenagers. Instead he asked me to meet with an older group. I went along a good number of times and then he was moved away from Targu Mures and the meetings stopped.

I met many interesting people through Levente and began to realise that Christians weren't old fashioned and didn't live in another world. Eventually I reached a stage where I thought Christianity made sense and decided that faith really worked for believers, but I couldn't believe. What I needed was proof to make sense of it all. That was towards the end of high school when I was eighteen years old.

No Free Choice

There was a system for those of us who wanted to go
to university and it was quite difficult to be accepted.
My parents had sent me to a school which focused on
mathematics and physics, though in those days nobody ever
asked what you wanted to become when you grew up. The
best students from my school went on to become maths
and physics teachers. But I wasn't one of the outstanding
students and I was told that I should become a construction
engineer or a mechanical engineer. At that time we were

informed by our schools what we were to do; we did not have a free choice.

I took the exam to study mechanical engineering and was selected. The stakes were quite high to get into a university with military service because if you did, you only served nine months before becoming an officer, well not quite an officer. What happened was that, in the case of mobilisation, you would immediately be advanced to lieutenant. Our rank would be sub-lieutenant. If you didn't make it to university, military service was two months training and then hard labour for another sixteen months. So it mattered quite a lot.

Him or Me

That's how I came to be in the army in Brasov in December 1989 when the revolution happened. I was eighteen years old and found myself caught in a gun fight with one of the guns in my hand. This is what happened. We were handed live ammunition and our lieutenant, who was twenty-three, gathered us for a briefing.

'If ordered, you have to shoot,' we were told. 'It's better that his or her mother cries rather than your mother.'

He turned to me and said, 'Do you understand, Csiszer?' I heard myself say that I didn't think I could shoot innocent people.

'Right Csiszer,' barked the lieutenant, 'you stay right next to me all the time and I will personally watch you.'

My colleagues, who were eighteen-year-olds like me, all felt the same as I did. 'Lieutenant,' said one, 'I will have to stand right next to Csiszer because I feel the same.' And then other voices joined in, saying, 'Me too,' 'And me too,' and 'Me too.' It was really intense.

Thanks to God's goodness (though I didn't know that then) we were not ordered to go out against the demonstrators.

The following night, when the shooting really started in Brasov against the so-called terrorists, we were marched out into action. It was chaos. It was the kind of total chaos that took us over. It didn't cross my mind whether God existed or not when I fired my weapon. We wanted to shoot at the vehicles coming towards us. To be totally honest, I didn't feel bad. I just fired.

We were due to finish military service at the end of June but, because of all the changes that followed the revolution, the authorities decided not to complete our training and released us. After a six month break, it was time for my

first classes in Cluj. That summer, through the influence of my girlfriend, I went to a Christian camp. It was run by Americans and I went because I'd studied English but had never had an opportunity to use the language. I thought it would be good to try it out. I really liked the community feeling, the songs and the whole atmosphere of the camp, but I didn't become a Christian. Then when college started, I began to attend a students' Bible study group and that's where I met Levente again. He was in Cluj by then.

Something Still Missing

The following summer, that was 1991, I attended the same camp and that was the first time I prayed to God saying I wanted to become a Christian and asking him to reveal himself to me. I don't know what I expected to happen, but it felt as if nothing changed. Later the Americans told me that, when they went home, in the American way they had to give a report back to their congregation about how many had been converted and I was the only one. It wasn't a very big success story for their church.

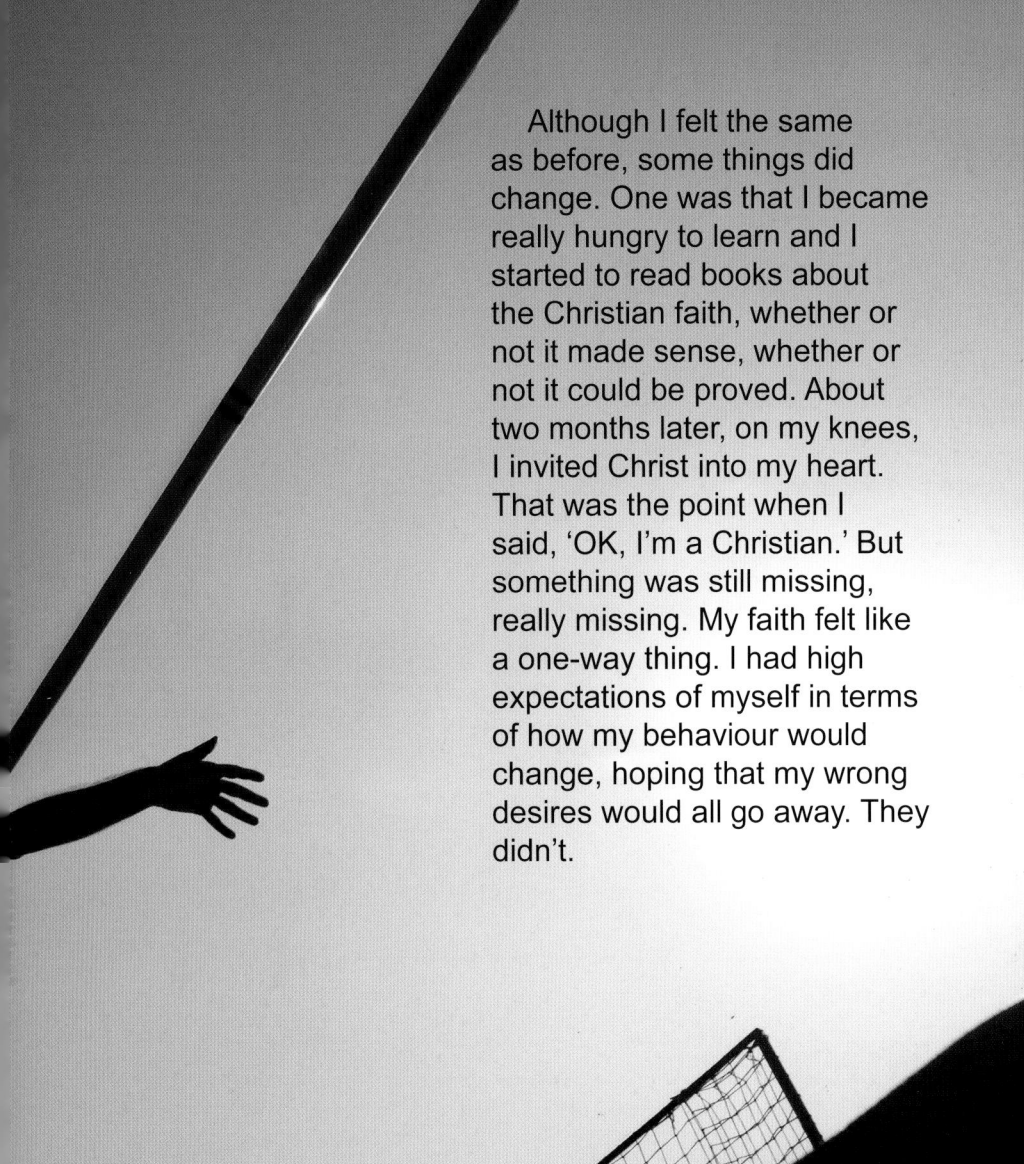

Although I felt the same as before, some things did change. One was that I became really hungry to learn and I started to read books about the Christian faith, whether or not it made sense, whether or not it could be proved. About two months later, on my knees, I invited Christ into my heart. That was the point when I said, 'OK, I'm a Christian.' But something was still missing, really missing. My faith felt like a one-way thing. I had high expectations of myself in terms of how my behaviour would change, hoping that my wrong desires would all go away. They didn't.

At that time I didn't feel that my sins were forgiven. It didn't click even though I was trying really hard. I called myself a Christian and really struggled to live up to the standards I thought were demanded of me. That was for about a year and a half. I didn't take part in Communion despite going to church.

One Sunday I was sitting in the upper floor of the church watching everyone taking Communion and I've never felt so lonely in my life. I'd had lonely moments before, and even do today, but I've never again felt how I felt that day. I decided it was simple. I'd be baptised and confirmed. Then I'd take Communion and my temptations would stop.

The Crucial Question

I decided to speak to a mature Christian and we talked and talked. I told him about my problems, temptations and sins. After some time he said, 'It's OK. Stop now. Do you believe that Christ died for your sins?' He stopped me focusing on my temptations and on my sins and made me focus on Christ. After that I was baptised and had to give my testimony. I didn't elaborate on my sins and shortcomings. But later that night I still felt frustrated. I still didn't feel different. But on the way home, as I thought things through, something clicked and I suddenly realised that no matter how hard we try, we don't qualify. That was the first time I felt what the forgiveness of sins is. And that was the moment from which I called myself a Christian. I knew then what relief was and peace. It had taken me about three years to reach that stage. It was a long time.

(Taken from *Wonderful! Blythswood People Share Stories of God's Faithfulness* by Irene Howat, Christian Focus Publications, 2016)

The Tax-collector's Story – the Sinner's Prayer

He [Jesus] also told this parable to some who trusted in themselves that they were righteous, and treated others with contempt:

"Two men went up into the temple to pray, one a Pharisee and the other a tax collector.

The Pharisee, standing by himself, prayed thus: 'God, I thank you that I am not like other men, extortioners, unjust, adulterers, or even like this tax collector.

I fast twice a week; I give tithes of all that I get.'

But the tax collector, standing far off, would not even lift up his eyes to heaven, but beat his breast, saying, 'God, be merciful to me, a sinner!'

I tell you, this man went down to his house justified, rather than the other. For everyone who exalts himself will be humbled, but the one who humbles himself will be exalted."

(Taken from the Gospel according to Luke, chapter 18 verses 10 to 14.)

How About You?

I can guess how that tax-collector felt. Like me, he wanted to be accepted by God. Jesus tells us that is exactly what happened. He went home justified, not because he had done something good but because he had thrown himself on God's mercy. The day that happened to me, I had joy, relief and the greatest sense of freedom.

You have read my story, and the story of the tax collector. How about you? We all need to have our sins forgiven by God, to be accepted by him. Every human being struggles with inner needs that only God can satisfy. Your weaknesses, your failures, your unfulfilled promises – God can take them all away and give you peace.

Make this your prayer today: God, be merciful to me, a sinner! For the sake of Jesus, Amen.

Blythswood Care

Education, Community, Gospel

Working from its base in the Highlands of Scotland, Blythswood Care is transforming the lives of children and adults in Europe, Africa and Asia. Education is one primary goal, bringing opportunities to disadvantaged children and young people. Community is another, with projects that extend help to people marginalised by poverty or prejudice. Gospel underpins both objectives, giving practical expression to the Christian beliefs that have motivated this organisation for more than 50 years.

Blythswood assists Christians and non-Christians alike, believing that everyone is precious in God's sight. Blythswood shares the gospel at every opportunity, believing it is for everyone – *For God so loved the world, that he gave his only Son, that whoever believes in him should not perish but have eternal life.* (John 3:16)

Head Office: Highland Deephaven, Evanton, Ross-shire, Scotland, IV16 9XJ

www.blythswood.org

Scottish charity SC021848

info@blythswood.org